HOW TO IDENTIFY WAR PLANES—
FRIEND OR ENEMY

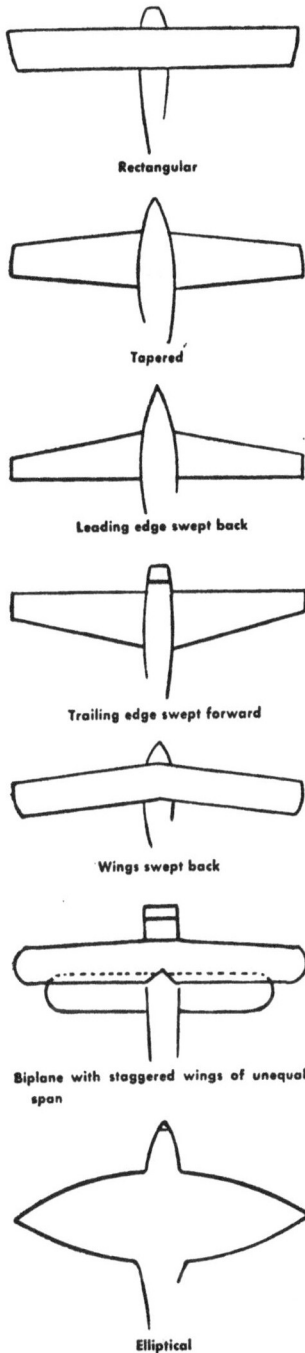

Rectangular

Tapered

Leading edge swept back

Trailing edge swept forward

Wings swept back

Biplane with staggered wings of unequal span

Elliptical

Figure 1

[*Note: In making this book available to the public, the Richfield Oil Corporation of New York has revealed no information which would be of aid to the enemies of our country. All items included in the contents have been compiled from established, trustworthy sources and constitute general information designed to aid the layman in identifying friendly and hostile aircraft.*]

Identifying airplanes may seem at first a job for an expert. Actually the various models of planes differ from one another in appearance more than automobile models. You can best learn to identify them by separating them first into broad classifications and then looking for the combination of special features that identifies the particular plane.

For purposes of identification, there are three useful general classifications for all planes: (1) land planes and sea planes; (2) monoplanes and biplanes; (3) single-engine planes and multi-engine planes.

Land planes and sea planes. Planes that take off from and land on water have either the large, boat-bottomed hull of the flying boat type of sea plane, or else they are conspicuous by the pontoons (usually two) that project below the wings or fuselage. In either case their general appearance is easily distinguishable from that of a plane that lands on a solid surface.

Monoplanes and biplanes. This classification is an easy one to make. However, the biplane is a disappearing type in combat planes, and except for a few special-purpose biplanes and some obsolescent models, combat planes are of the monoplane type.

Single-engine and multi-engine planes. The number of engines on a plane is easy to note. Of the multi-engine planes, two-motor planes and four-motor planes are the commonest. The three-motor plane a prevalent type ten years ago, has practically disappeared except in the Italian air force.

By classifying the plane you see in these three easy ways you can considerably narrow your search for its identity. Next you need to know where to look to see the distinguishing features in appearance that complete the identification. Here are the points to observe:

(1) *Shape and attachment of wings.* The plan of the wings (the wing shape that you see when the plane is directly overhead) shows wide variation in different planes. In Figure 1 note the way of describing the different wing plans.

In the head-on view of the plane, there is a similar variation in their outline (see Figure 2) and in the place of their attachment to the fuselage (body of the plane) (see Figure 3). In the case of a biplane, you should also note whether the two wings are of equal span (distance from tip to tip) or whether the lower wing has a shorter span than the upper, and whether they are unstaggered or staggered. A biplane's wings are said to be staggered when the lower wing is set further to the rear than the upper. There are a few biplanes with a "negative" stagger, in which the lower wing is set forward of the upper.

(2) *Tail assemblage.* The tail assemblage of a plane consists of a horizontal tailplane, with a movable rear section called the elevator, and a vertical plane (or planes) called the fin, with a movable rear section, the rudder. Most single-engine planes have a single fin and rudder, but one of the first things to observe in a multi-engine plane is whether it has a single fin and rudder or two fins and rudders mounted at, or near, the ends of the tailplane (see Figure 4). The tailplane plans of aircraft vary as greatly as wing plans, and the fin and rudder frequently have an identifying shape.

(3) *Shape of the fuselage.* The shape of the fuselage can vary all the way from the short "barrel" fuselages of certain fighters to the elongated, tapered fuselages of some bomber models. Sometimes a bomber's fuselage will be sharply stepped down or stepped up just behind the wings to allow for rear gunner stations. The length and shape of the nose, the part of the fuselage that projects forward of the wings, is frequently characteristic. Gun turrets, in the nose, on top of the fuselage, or in the tail, are also identifying features.

(4) *Shape and attachment of the engines.* The air-cooled, radial engine with its cowling presents a flat forward surface, which contrasts sharply with the streamlining that the in-line, liquid-cooled engine makes possible. In multi-engine planes the engine nacelles (engine housing) are sometimes underslung on the wings, sometimes centered, and occasionally mounted on top of the wings. In a few models the engine nacelles project behind the trailing edges of the wings.

With all these points of variation, you will find that each plane has its particular group of special features that point to its exact identity. In this book you will find descriptions, drawings and brief "ways to identify" each plane. When you have studied them, you can test your knowledge with the airplane shots you see in newspapers, magazines, and at the movies. If you have a reasonably good eye you will find that "spotting" airplanes in the air becomes easier with practice.

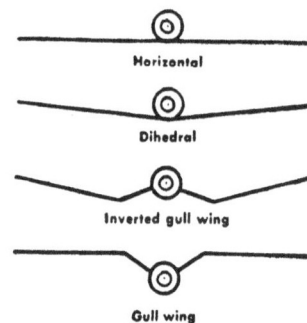

Horizontal

Dihedral

Inverted gull wing

Gull wing

Figure 2

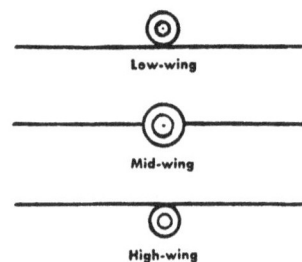

Low-wing

Mid-wing

High-wing

Figure 3

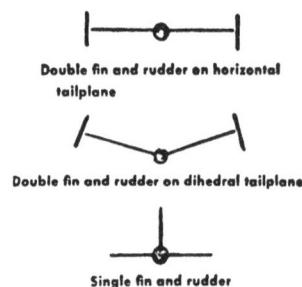

Double fin and rudder on horizontal tailplane

Double fin and rudder on dihedral tailplane

Single fin and rudder

Figure 4

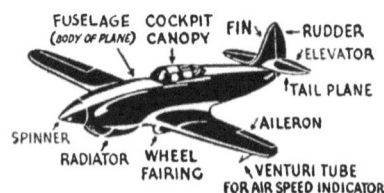

FUSELAGE (BODY OF PLANE) — COCKPIT CANOPY — FIN — RUDDER — ELEVATOR — TAIL PLANE — AILERON — VENTURI TUBE FOR AIR SPEED INDICATOR — WHEEL FAIRING — RADIATOR — SPINNER

FRIENDLY PLANES
UNITED STATES

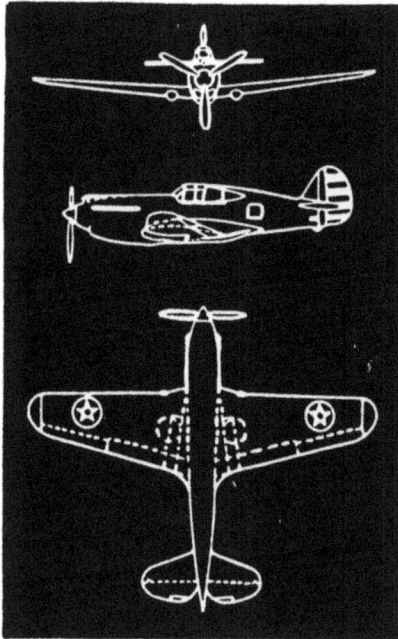

The Curtiss P-40, called the "Tomahawk" in the R.A.F., a single-place fighter powered by a liquid-cooled in-line Allison engine of 950-hp. Its top speed is around 350 m.p.h. Machine guns fire through propeller area. Further data restricted.

Way to Identify—Low-wing monoplane with dihedral wings untapered on leading edges and swept forward on trailing edges to rounded tips. Small "knees" under wings near fuselage. Long nose, streamlined fuselage. Tailplane mounted high, single fin and rudder.

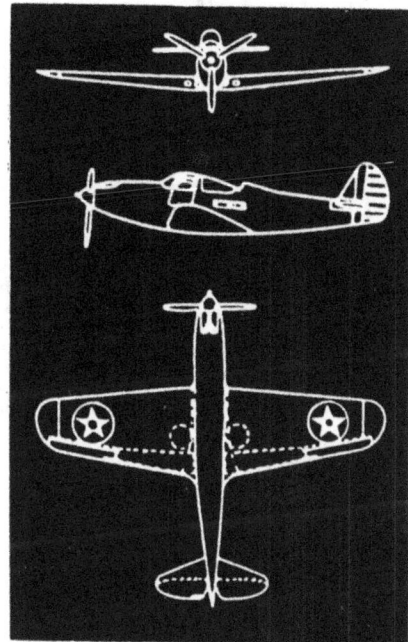

The Bell P-39 "Airacobra," a single-seat fighter powered by a 1,050-hp. Allison engine behind the cockpit driving the propeller through an extension drive shaft. A speed of 400 m.p.h. makes it one of the Army's fastest. A 37-mm. cannon fires through propeller hub, and it has additional 30- and 50-calibre machine guns. It has a retractable tricycle landing gear.

Way to Identify—Low-wing monoplane, with dihedral wings tapered to rounded tips. Long nose, cleanly streamlined. Leading edges of tailplane swept back. Single fin and rudder.

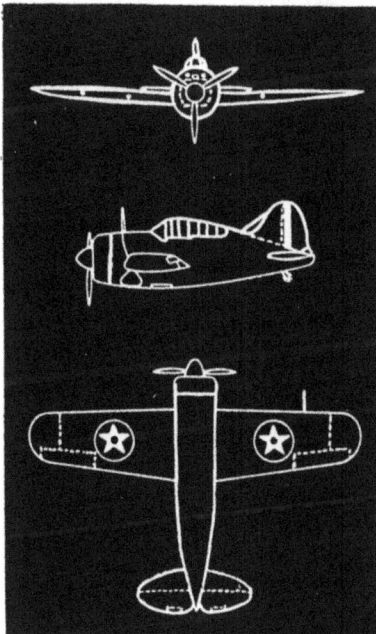

The Brewster "Buffalo," a one-seater fighter with a top speed of approximately 350 m.p.h., powered by a 1,200-hp. Wright "Cyclone" radial engine. This ship was developed from the Navy's F2A-2 fighter, and is reported to have the unusual fighter range of 1,500 miles.

Way to Identify — Low mid-wing monoplane with slightly tapered wings of short span and rounded tips. Stubby "barrel" fuselage. Elliptical tailplane, single fin and rudder.

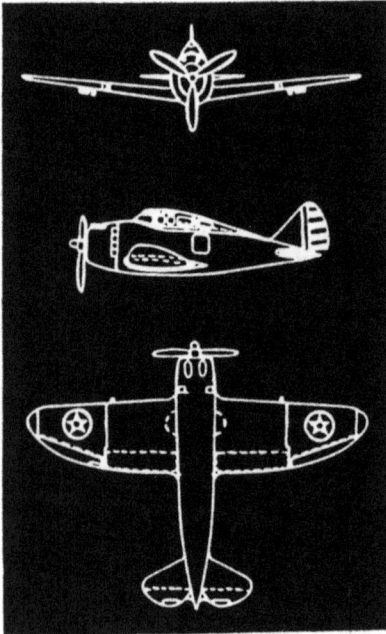

The Republic P-43 "Lancer," a single-place fighter equipped with 30- and 50-calibre wing guns and light fragmentation bombs, and powered by a 1,100-hp. Pratt & Whitney "Twin Wasp" radial engine. No data on performance.
Way to Identify—Low-wing monoplane with dihedral wings untapered on leading edges and curved forward on trailing edges. Tailplane mounted low, single fin and rudder.

The Grumman F4F-3, christened the "Wildcat" in the Navy, a single-place fighter powered either by a Wright or a Pratt & Whitney radial engine, built for aircraft carrier service. This ship was developed from the Grumman G-36A. Further data restricted.
Way to Identify—Mid-wing monoplane with wings slightly tapered to square-cut tips. Short cylindrical fuselage. Tailplane of angular cut mounted high on single fin and rudder.

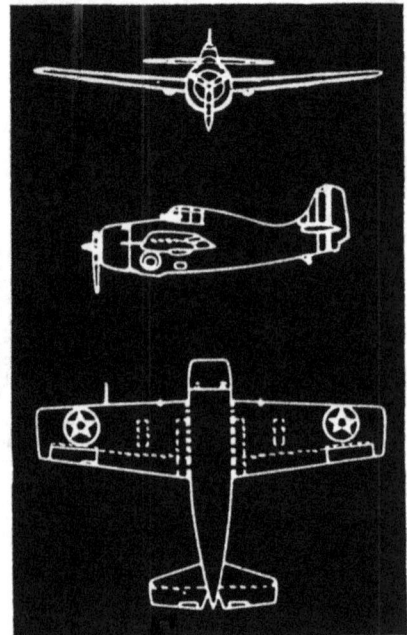

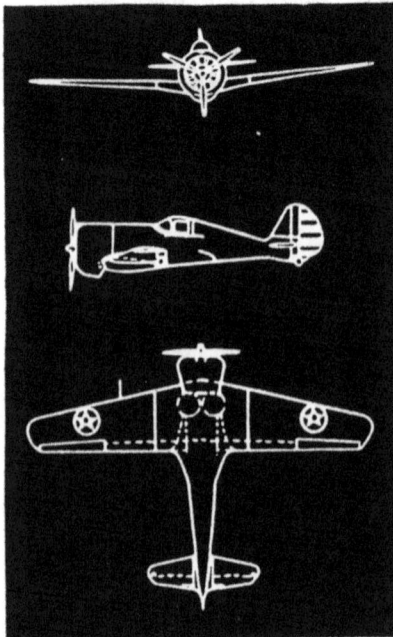

The Curtiss-Wright 21-B, a single-seat fighter powered by a Wright 850-hp. "Cyclone" radial engine, and armed with four machine guns in the wings. It has a top speed of 333 m.p.h. and a cruising range of 630 miles.
Way to Identify—Low-wing monoplane with dihedral wings, swept back on leading edges and untapered on trailing edges. Bottom of engine cowling projects below fuselage. High single fin and rudder.

4

The Vought-Sikorsky SB2U-1, the Navy's "Vindicator," a two-place scout and dive bomber for aircraft carrier service. It has a top speed of 260 m.p.h. and cruising range of over 725 miles, and is powered by a Pratt & Whitney "Twin Wasp, Jr." radial engine of 750-hp. The export version of this ship is called The "Chesapeake" in England.

Way to Identify—Low-wing monoplane, with wings slightly tapered to rounded tips, dihedral on outer sections. Long thin fuselage with tapered tailplane and single fin and rudder.

The Vultee P-48 "Vanguard," a single-place fighter with a top speed of 345 m.p.h. and a cruising range of 1,190 miles. Armed with two synchronized machine guns and powered by a 1,200-hp. Pratt & Whitney radial engine.

Way to Identify — Low-wing monoplane, with wings almost equally tapered and semicircular tips. Tailplane of similar plan and high fin and rudder.

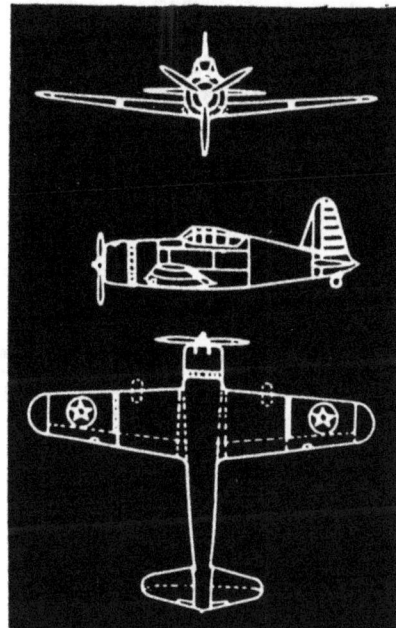

The North American P-51 "Apache," a single-seater fighter powered by an Allison 1,000-hp. engine. This ship is known as the "Mustang" in the R.A.F.

Way to Identify — Low-wing monoplane with marked dihedral, and wings almost equally tapered. Long nose. Rectangular tailplane mounted high and long, thin fuselage.

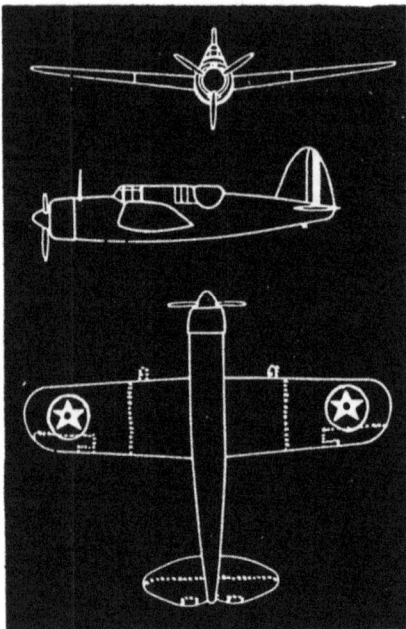

The Brewster SB2A-1, the Navy's "Bucanneer," a high-speed, two-seater, long-range dive bomber, carries a 1,000-lb bomb inside fuselage, and has a power-operated turret at the rear of the fuselage. It is powered by a 1,700-hp. Wright "Cyclone" engine. Reported to be more than 100 m.p.h. faster than the German "Stuka." Export version is called the "Bermuda."
Way to Identify—Mid-wing monoplane, with dihedral wings slightly tapered to rounded tips. Long fuselage with gun turret between the back of wing and tail assembly. Elliptical tailplane and high curved fin and rudder.

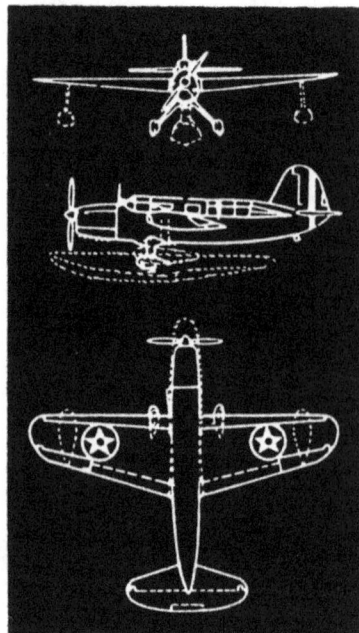

The Curtiss SO3C-1, the Navy's "Seagull," a two-seater scout and observation plane equipped either as a land or carrier-based plane, or as a seaplane, with a single pontoon below fuselage and two wing floats. Powered by a 520-hp. Ranger engine.
Way to Identify — Mid-wing monoplane, with leading edges untapered and trailing edges swept forward. Fixed undercarriage, or large center pontoon and wing floats. Elliptical tailplane and large curved single fin and rudder.

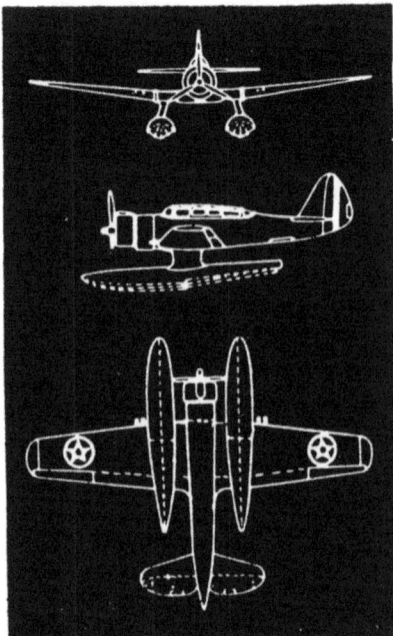

The Northrop N-3PB, a three-place patrol seaplane, powered by a Wright "Cyclone" radial engine. Top speed is over 225 m.p.h.
Way to Identify—Low-wing monoplane with slight dihedral and tapered wings. Two pontoons and no wing floats Tailplane high and large fin.

6

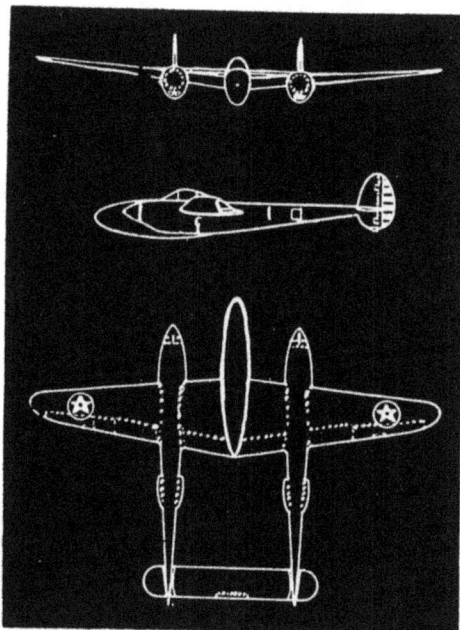

The Lockheed P-38 "Lightning," a single-place, two-engine fighter of unusual design. Two 1,050-hp. Allison engines give it a top speed of over 400 m.p.h. and a cruising range of over 1,000 miles. Armed with a 37-mm. cannon and four machine guns in nose. Tricycle landing gear.

Way to Identify — Monoplane with tapered wings. Slender tail booms behind each engine carry tailplane between them, with double fins and rudders. Pilot's nacelle extends far forward and does not extend behind wing.

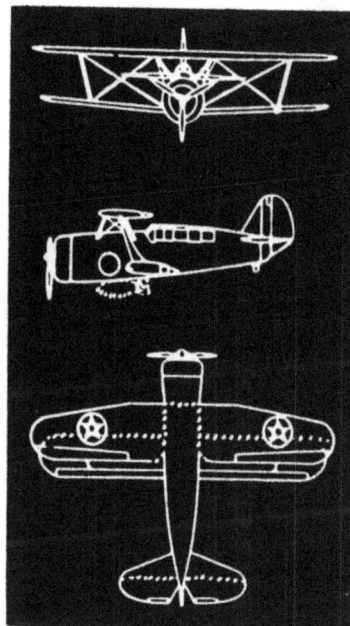

The Curtiss SBC-4, a two-place scout and dive bomber, is no longer in production, but is still being used. Armed with one fixed machine gun and one flexibly mounted gun in rear cockpit, and carries bombs externally. It has a speed of 235 m.p.h. and a range of 850 miles. Powered by 850-hp. Wright "Cyclone" engine. (R.A.F. "Cleveland").

Way to Identify—Biplane with staggered wings and upper wings of slightly greater span. Single struts. Fuselage short and thick.

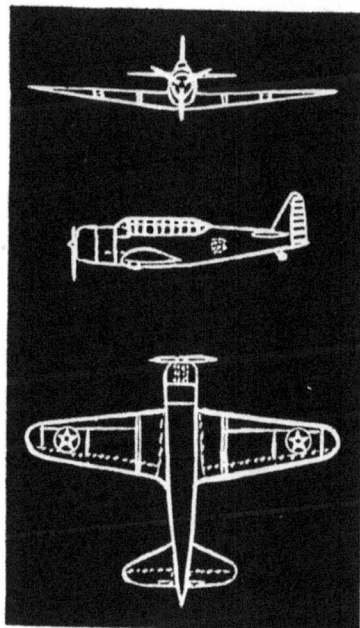

The Vultee V-12C, an attack bomber with a crew of three, armed with two fixed forward guns and upper and lower flexible-mount guns in rear cockpit. Carries large bombs externally and small bombs internally. Top speed over 250 m.p.h. and cruising range 2,400 miles with 900-hp. Wright radial engine.

Way to Identify—Low-wing monoplane, with tapered wings. Long fuselage tapering to point with tailplane mounted high. Elliptical single fin and rudder.

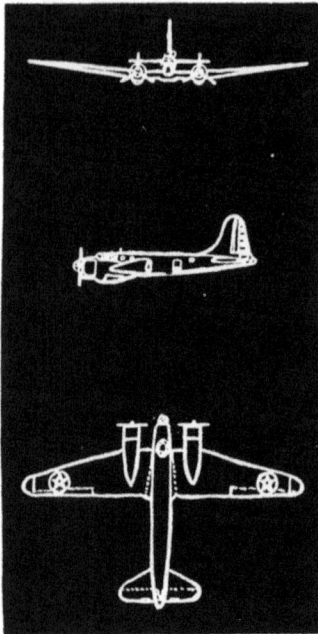

The Douglas B-23, a two-engine bomber and reconnaissance plane. This ship is an improved version of the Army's B-18 bomber. All data on performance and equipment is restricted.

Way to Identify – Low-wing monoplane with leading edges swept back from engine nacelles and untapered trailing edges. Nose tip and propellers on approximately the same line. Engine nacelles do not project behind wings. Swept-back tailplane. Very high single fin and rudder.

The Douglas B-18, a twin-engine bomber powered by two Wright "Cyclone" engines and said to have a speed of over 225 m.p.h. It has internal bomb compartment and gun positions in the nose and above and below the fuselage behind the wings.

Way to Identify — Mid-wing monoplane, with wings swept back on leading edges, trailing edges straight, slight dihedral on outer edges, fuselage long and deep with transparent nose; swept back tailplane with large single fin and rudder.

The Douglas A-20, known in the R.A.F. as the "Havoc," an attack bomber, with a three-man crew, powered by two 1,600-hp. Wright "Cyclone" engines. Official data restricted, but it is believed to have the unusual bomber speed of over 315 m.p.h, and to carry over a ton of bombs. Reported used as a night fighter in England.

Way to Identify – High mid-wing monoplane, with leading edges untapered and trailing edges swept forward to narrow tips. Engine nacelles project behind wings and nose projects far forward of wings. Elliptical tailplane. Very high single fin and rudder.

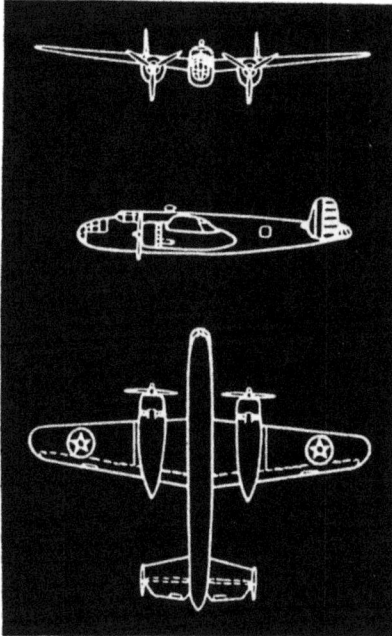

The North American B-25, a medium bomber with a crew of five, a top speed of about 300 m.p.h. and a cruising range of over 2,600 miles. Powered by two Wright "Cyclone" 1,600-hp. radial engines.
Way to Identify—Mid-wing monoplane with tapered wings. Engine nacelles underslung, projecting slightly behind wings. Very long nose and thin, deep fuselage with double fins and rudders.

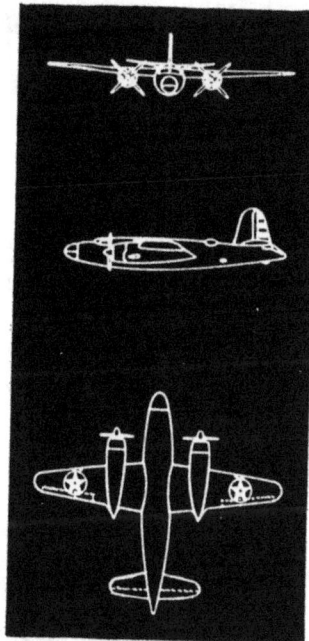

The Martin B-26, a medium bomber, one of the latest types in quantity production. Powered by two 1,850-hp. Pratt & Whitney radial engines equipped with four-bladed propellers, it is heavily armed and carries a large bomb load, and is said to be faster and deadlier than most fighter types. It carries a "stinger" turret in the tail. Official data restricted.
Way to Identify—High-wing monoplane, with fully tapered wings. Round transparent nose projects well forward of engines, and cylindrical fuselage projects beyond tall single tail fin and rudder.

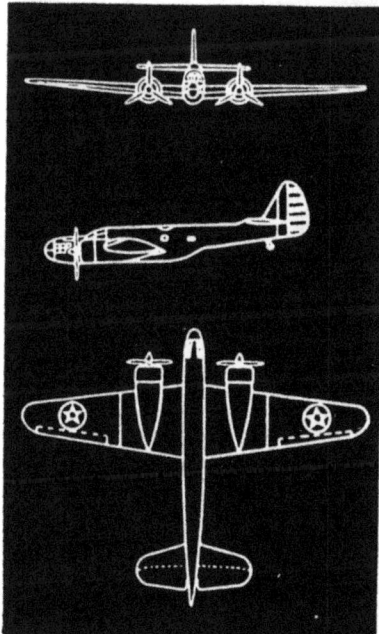

The Martin 167W, a bomber and reconnaissance plane with a crew of three. It has a top speed of over 300 m.p.h. and range of almost 2,500 miles, powered by two Pratt & Whitney "Twin Wasp" engines. This plane is called the "Maryland" in Great Britain, and it has performed well in the Mediterranean.
Way to Identify—Low mid-wing monoplane with tapered wings. Engine nacelles project behind wing. Nose well forward of engines. Long thin fuselage, extremely deep on underside behind wings. Elliptical tailplane and single fin and rudder.

9

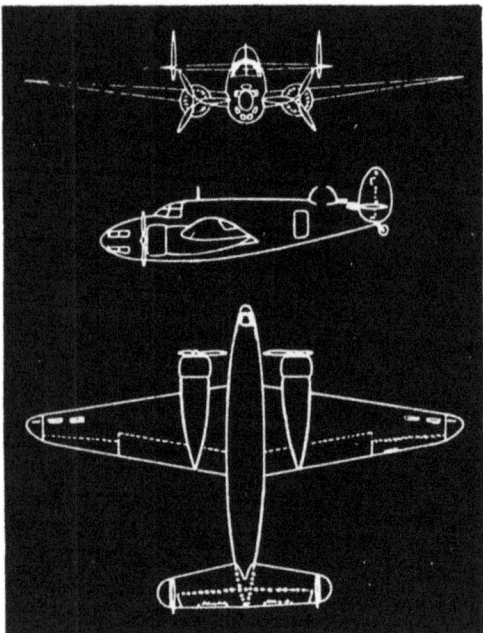

The Lockheed "Hudson," well known for its service in the R.A.F. Costal Command, is a four-place bomber and reconnaissance plane. It is powered by two Wright "Cyclone" engines, and its armament includes a power-operated turret in rear of fuselage. These planes can be ferried to England from Canada in ten hours and under.

Way to Identify—Low mid-wing monoplane with fully tapered wings. Thin, deep fuselage tapering to tail-plane of wide span, mounting two fins and rudders of egg-shaped profile. Gun turret in rear of fuselage.

The Martin PBM-1, the Navy's "Mariner," a patrol bomber flying boat, carries a crew of seven. Powered by two Wright "Cyclone" engines of 1,350-hp. each. Gun mounts are located in nose, on top, both sides and underside of rear of fuselage.

Way to Identify—High-wing monoplane of "gull wing" type. Wide span with full taper. Large two-step hull tapering to high tailplane with full dihedral mounting double fins and rudders.

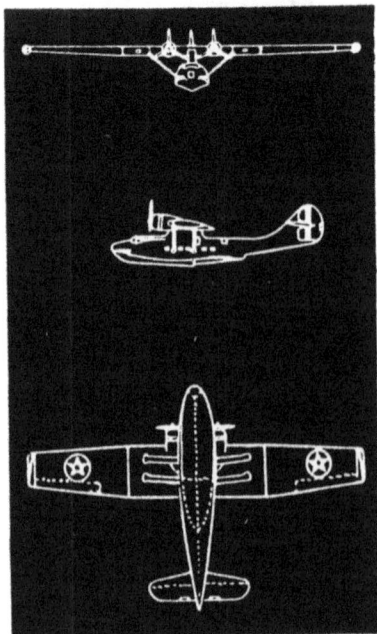

The Consolidated PBY-5 "Catalina," the long-range patrol bomber flying boat that spotted the raider *Bismarck* for the British Navy. Powered by two Pratt & Whitney "Twin Wasp" engines, it has a great cruising range. Further data restricted.

Way to Identify—High-wing monoplane with wings tapered on outer sections and square-cut tips (formed by retracted wing floats). Two-step hull, fuselage tapering to single tail fin with tailplane mounted high on it.

The Consolidated B-24, "Liberator," a four-engine heavy bomber. This model, with the "Flying Fortress" models, is the backbone of the Army's heavy-bomber building program now under way. Powered by four 1,200-hp. Pratt & Whitney engines, it has a top speed of 300 m.p.h., a range of over 3,000 miles, and is reported to carry about four tons of bombs.
Way to Identify—High-wing monoplane, with wings of wide span and full taper. Top line of fuselage sweeps straight back to rectangular tailplane with rounded double fins and rudders.

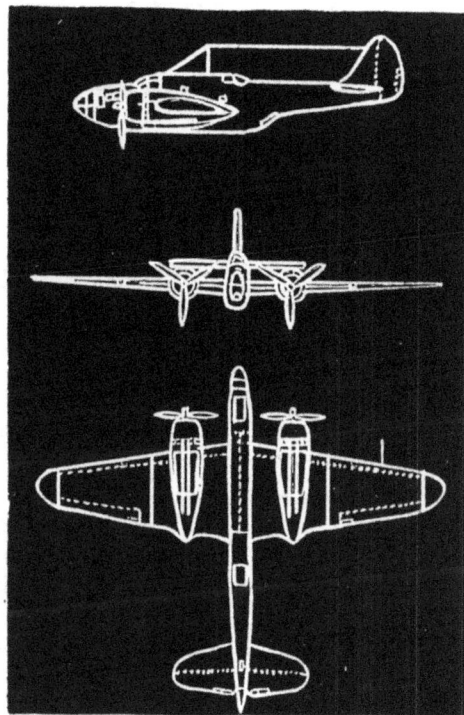

The Martin 187, the R.A.F.'s "Baltimore," a medium bomber powered by two Wright radial engines of 1,600-hp. each. It is reported to be one of the fastest bombers in its class in the world, designed on the basis of experience gained by the R.A.F. Bomber Command. It carries heavy offensive and defensive armament, including a power-operated gun turret.
Way to Identify—Mid-wing monoplane with tapered wings and rounded tips. Engine nacelles somewhat underslung. Deep-waisted fuselage with pointed transparent nose. Tapered tailplane, single fin and rudder.

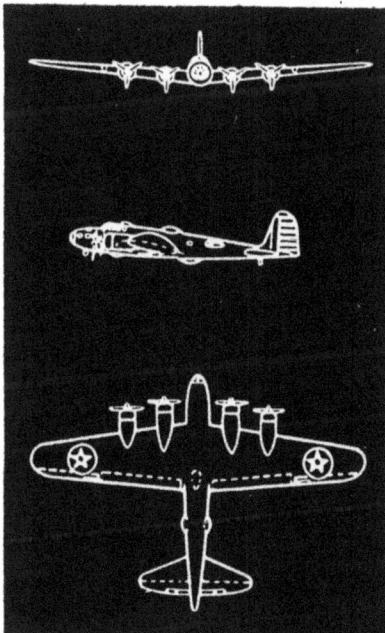

The Boeing B-17 "Flying Fortress," a development of the B-15, which pioneered in the field of the long-range heavy bomber. Powered by four 1,200-hp. Wright "Cyclone" engines, it is reported to have a top speed of around 300 m.p.h. and a range of over 3,500 miles.
Way to Identify—Low-wing monoplane, with dihedral wings, with leading edges swept back and trailing edges slightly swept forward. Inner pair of engines forward of outer pair, and nose well forward of inner engines. Tapered tailplane and high, rounded single fin and rudder.

GREAT BRITAIN

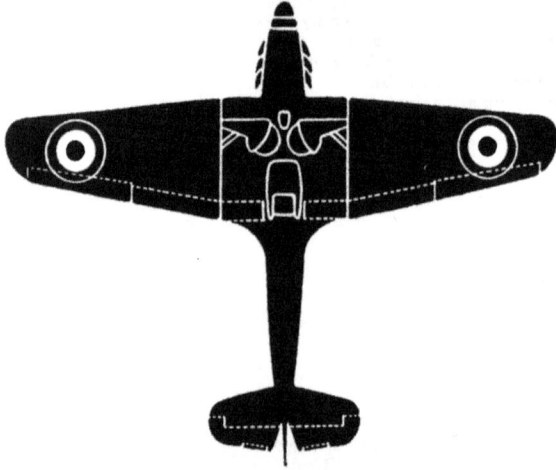

The Hawker "Hurricane," companion fighter to the "Spitfire," a single-seat fighter armed with eight machine guns in the wings and powered by a Rolls-Royce "Merlin" in-line engine of 1,030-hp. This model has a speed of about 350 m.p.h., but newest version is reported much faster and armed with either twelve machine guns or four cannon. *Way to Identify*—Low-wing monoplane with inner sections of wings horizontal and outer sections at slight dihedral angle. Wing plan almost equally tapered on both leading and trailing edges to rounded tips. Large single fin and rudder. Radiator projects under fuselage.

The Supermarine "Spitfire," England's most famous fighter, with a top speed of approximately 380 m.p.h., and armament of eight machine guns in the wings. Powered by a Rolls-Royce "Merlin" engine of 1,030-hp. An improved version is reported to have a speed around 400 m.p.h. and armament of cannon as well as machine guns. This ship and the "Hurricane" are the backbone of the R.A.F. Fighter Command.
Way to Identify—Low-wing monoplane with wings of marked dihedral. Wing plan and tailplane plan almost elliptical. Small fin and rudder. Radiator projects under left wing.

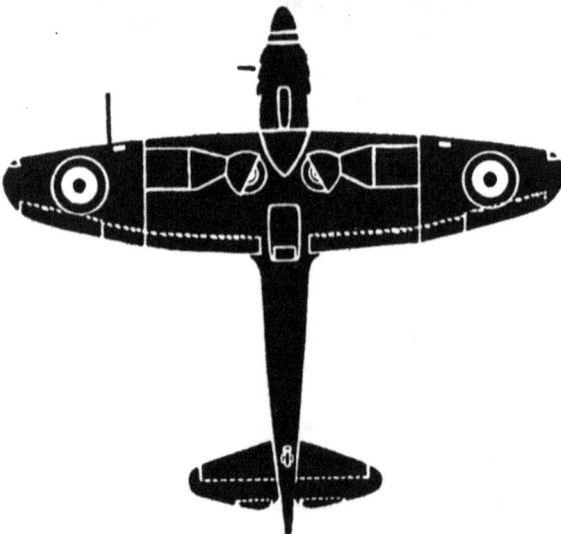

The Bolton-Paul "Defiant," a two-place fighter with a power-operated four-gun turret mounted behind the pilot's cockpit. One of the first fighter models to use a turret gun. It is powered by a Rolls-Royce "Merlin" engine of 1,030-hp. It is reported to be used as a night fighter. No data on performance available.
Way to Identify—Low-wing monoplane with wings dihedral on outer sections and almost equally tapered. Turret visible behind cockpit. Single triangular fin and rudder.

12

The Fairey "Fulmar," a two-place fighter for service on aircraft carriers. It has a Rolls-Royce "Merlin" engine of 1,145-hp. and eight machine guns in wings. Reported to be England's best naval fighter. No other information available.
Way to Identify—Low-wing monoplane with leading edges of wings sharply swept back and trailing edges swept back at smaller angle. Long nose and long fuselage tapered to a point. Tapered tailplane. Single fin and rudder.

The Blackburn "Skua," a fighter and dive bomber for fleet service with a crew of two, powered by a Bristol "Perseus" radial engine of 905-hp. It carries four machine guns in wings and an additional one in rear cockpit, plus a bomb load. Top speed of 225 m.p.h.
Way to Identify—Low-wing monoplane with horizontal wings tipped up at wing tips. Wings tapered almost evenly to rounded tips. High elliptical single fin and rudder set forward of end of fuselage

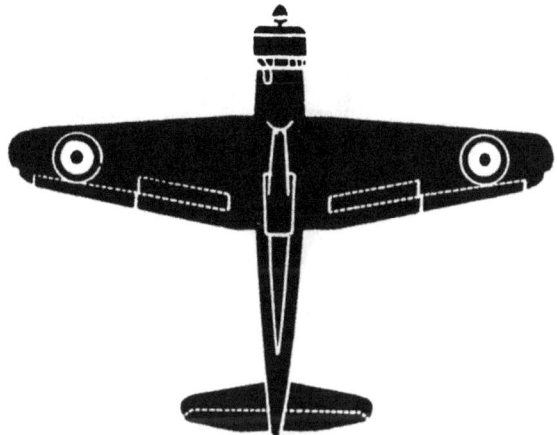

The Blackburn "Roc," a two-place fighter for fleet service. It carries a multi-gun turret behind pilot's cockpit. Powered by a Bristol "Perseus" radial engine. No further data available.
Way to Identify—Generally similar to the "Skua" except that the wings are not tipped up at the ends and turret replaces rear observation cockpit.

The Westland "Lysander," a two-seater all-pur-
pose plane, used for army cooperation. Powered
by a Bristol radial engine of 950-hp., it has a top
speed of 230 m.p.h. It mounts machine guns in
the landing wheel fairings and in the rear cockpit, and has racks for light bombs on stub wings
above landing wheels.
Way to Identify — High-wing monoplane with
leading edges untapered and trailing edges
swept forward on outer sections. Fixed undercarriage and diagonal struts between wings and
undercarriage. Large triangular single fin and
rudder.

The Avro "Anson," a two-engine reconnaissance
plane and bomber with a crew of four, in use for
patroling by the Costal Command. Powered by
two Armstrong-Siddeley "Cheetah" radial engines of 350-hp. each, it has a top speed of 188
m.p.h. It mounts a turret on top of fuselage.
Way to Identify — Low-wing monoplane with
wings slightly tapered to rounded tips. Fuselage
behind wings deep and thin. Tailplane of
diamond pattern mounted low. Single fin and
rudder.

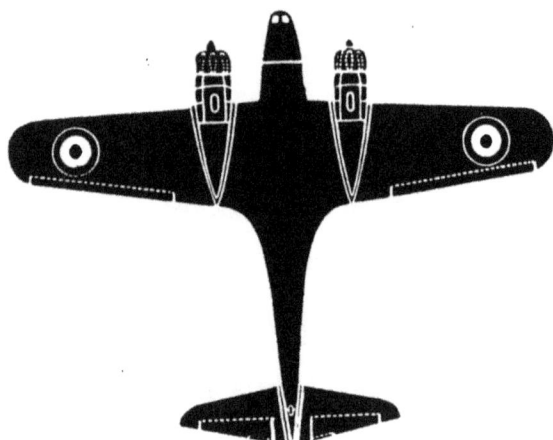

The Handley-Page "Hampden," a two-engine medium bomber which has played a prominent part
in raids over occupied France and the Ruhr. It
carries six machine guns in gun stations in the
nose and in the upper and lower rear fuselage.
Powered by two Bristol "Perseus" radial engines
of 980-hp. each, it has a top speed of 265 m.p.h.,
and a range of 1,725 miles. Accommodates a
crew of four.
Way to Identify — Mid-wing monoplane, with
leading edges of wings swept back slightly and
trailing edges swept forward sharply to narrow
rounded tips. From the rear gun stations the
fuselage continues as thin tail boom. Double fins
and rudders.

The Armstrong-Whitworth "Whitley," a twin-engine heavy bomber, fitted either with two radial engines of 845-hp. each or two liquid-cooled in-line engines of 1,030-hp. each. With the latter, it has a top speed of 245 m.p.h. and cruising range of 1,800 miles. It carries a normal crew of five, and has gun turrets in nose and tail, and carries bombs in fuselage and wings. This plane has been used extensively in night raiding over Germany.

Way to Identify — Mid-wing monoplane with broad wings slightly tapered. Long, straight, slab-sided fuselage projecting beyond rectangular tailplane. Double fins and rudders. Gun turret in tail.

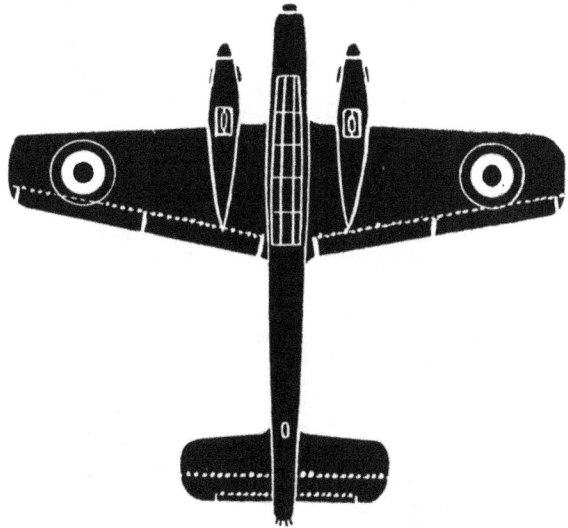

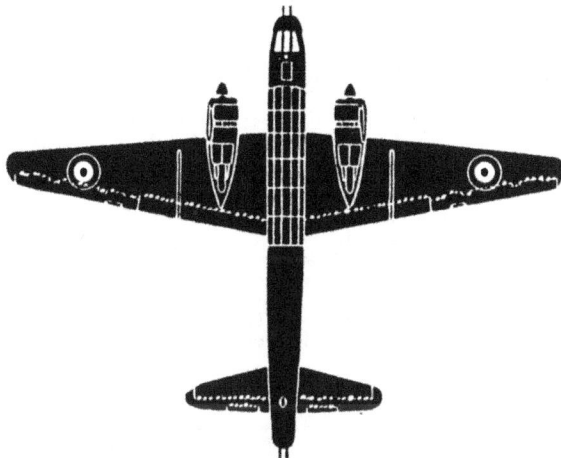

The Vicker's "Wellington," a heavy bomber with a maximum range of 3,200 miles and top speed of over 250 m.p.h. Extensively used for night bombings on Berlin and northern Italy. It has gun positions in the nose, in the fuselage amidships and in the tail. It accommodates a crew of five, and is powered either by two radial or two in-line engines.

Way to Identify—Mid-wing monoplane, with tapered wings of wide span. Long nose and deep, narrow, slab-sided fuselage projecting beyond tailplane. Tall single fin and rudder of triangular shape rounded at top.

The Bristol "Blenheim," a three-place medium bomber reported to have been used as a special night fighter. It is powered by two Bristol "Mercury" radial engines of 920-hp. each, and has a gun station in the nose and a retractable turret on top of the fuselage. Its top speed is 295 m.p.h. and its range about 2,000.

Way to Identify—High mid-wing monoplane with edges almost equally tapered to rounded tips. Fuselage thin and deep behind wings, and high single fin and rudder.

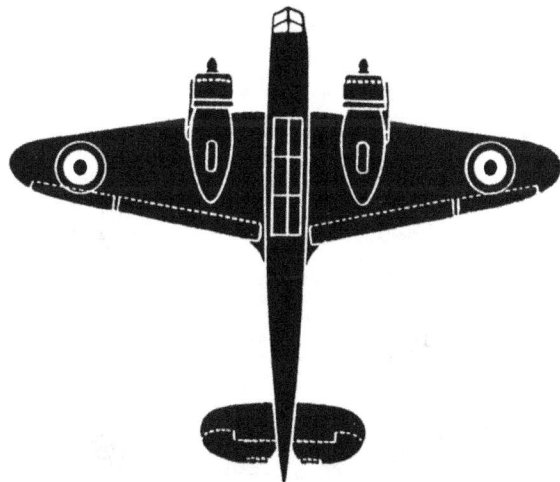

The Gloster "Gladiator," a one-seater fighter armed with four machine guns. This ship has been replaced by more modern fighters in the main combat area. It has a top speed of 250 m.p.h., and is powered by a Bristol "Mercury" radial engine of 825-hp.
Way to Identify—Biplane with staggered wings of equal span. Short nose with radial cowling. Fixed undercarriage. Elliptical tailplane and large, rounded fin and rudder.

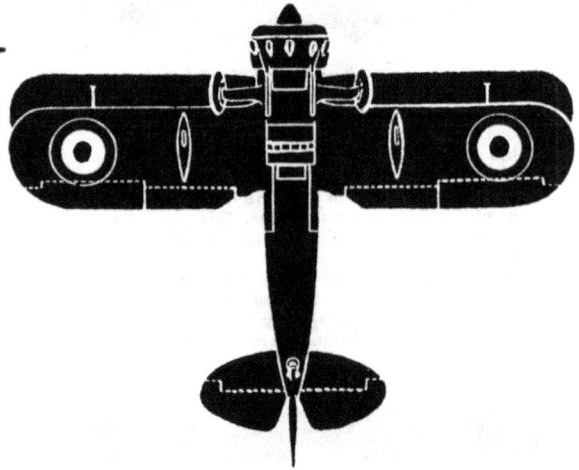

The Bristol "Beaufort," a four-crew bomber, reconnaissance and general-purpose plane. In use as a mine layer for the Costal Command. It is powered by two Bristol "Taurus" radial engines of 1,060-hp. each, and has machine gun stations in nose and in turret on fuselage. No data on performance available.
Way to Identify — Mid-wing monoplane, with wings horizontal on inner sections and set at dihedral angle outside of motors. Fuselage stepped down behind turret. Engines underslung. Tailplane mounted high, and single fin and rudder.

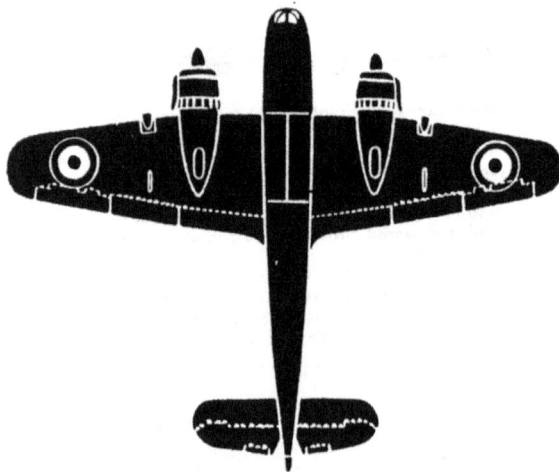

The Bristol "Bombay," a bomber and transport plane. Its top speed is 190 m.p.h., powered by two Bristol "Pegasus" radial engines of 890-hp. It carries a crew of four for bombing, and can transport twenty-four armed soldiers. Machine gun stations in nose and tail. It has a range of 2,230 miles.
Way to Identify—High-wing monoplane with fixed landing wheels attached by vertical posts to engine nacelles and diagonal struts to bottom of fuselage. Fuselage with tail turret projects well beyond tailplane mounting two fins and rudders.

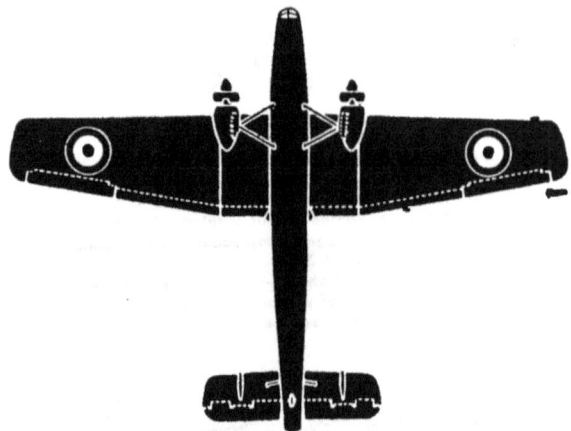

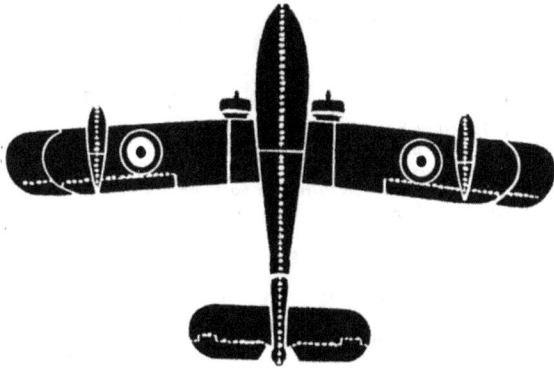

Supermarine "Stanraer," a flying boat for bombing and patrol, with a cruising range of 1,000 miles and a top speed of 165 m.p.h. Powered by two Bristol radial engines of 950-hp. each.

Way to Identify—Biplane with wings of unequal span, both wings equally swept back. Boat hull attached to lower wing and two engines mounted under top wing. Rectangular tailplane with semicircular tips mounting two fins and rudders.

The Fairey "Sea Fox," a two-seater reconnaissance catapult seaplane for cruiser and battleship use. Powered by a Napier "Rapier" in-line engine of 370-hp., it has a top speed of 125 m.p.h. This model is no longer in production but is still in service.

Way to Identify—Biplane with wings of equal span, slightly staggered. Wings rectangular and slightly swept back with square tips. Twin floats. Large single fin and rudder.

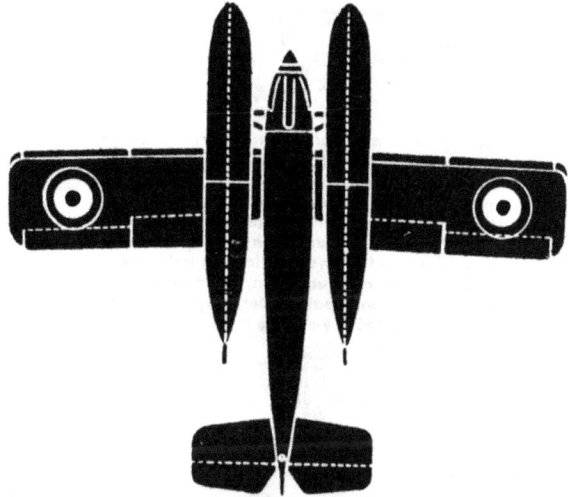

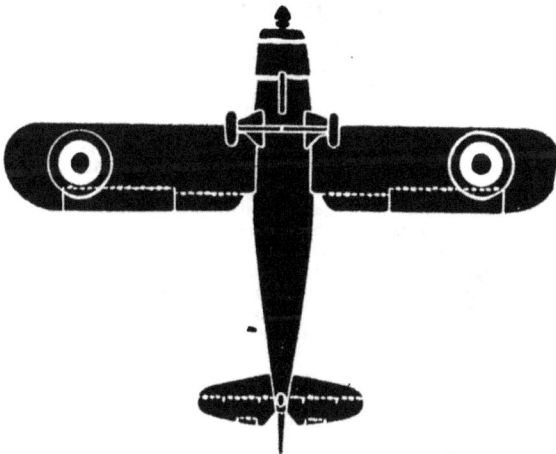

The Fairey "Albacore," a reconnaissance plane used as a fleet spotter, equipped either with landing wheels (as shown) for carrier service or with pontoons. It carries a crew of two or three, and has a top speed of around 200 m.p.h. Powered by a Bristol "Taurus" radial engine of 1,065-hp.

Way to Identify—Biplane with wings of equal span, unstaggered. Both wings set at slight dihedral. Fixed landing gear. Elliptical tailplane and single fin and rudder.

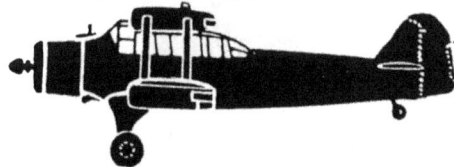

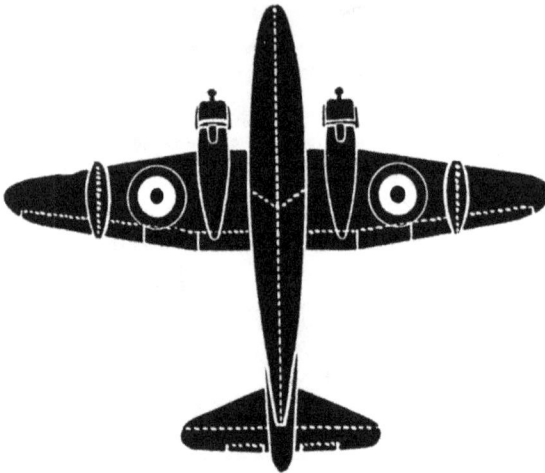

The *Saunders-Roe "Lerwick,"* a patrol bomber flying boat, powered by two Bristol "Hercules" radial engines of 1,375-hp. each. It carries a crew of seven and has gun turrets in nose, on top of fuselage and in tail. No data on performance
Way to Identify — High-wing monoplane with wings horizontal on inner sections, and outside sections with dihedral tapered sharply to almost pointed tips. Fixed wing floats. Very deep hull with triangular tailplane mounted high and high single fin and rudder.

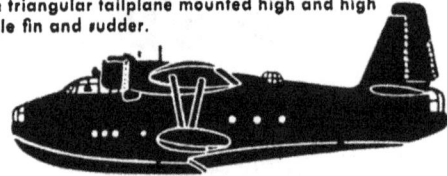

The *Supermarine "Walrus,"* an amphibian reconnaissance flying boat with a crew of five, used chiefly as a submarine spotter. Its Bristol radial engine powers a pusher-type propeller. It has a speed of 135 m.p.h. and range of 600 miles.
Way to Identify — Biplane with hull carried below lower plane and engine nacelle mounted between planes. Wings of equal span, unstaggered and swept back. Wing floats under wing struts. Tailplane mounted high on single fin and rudder.

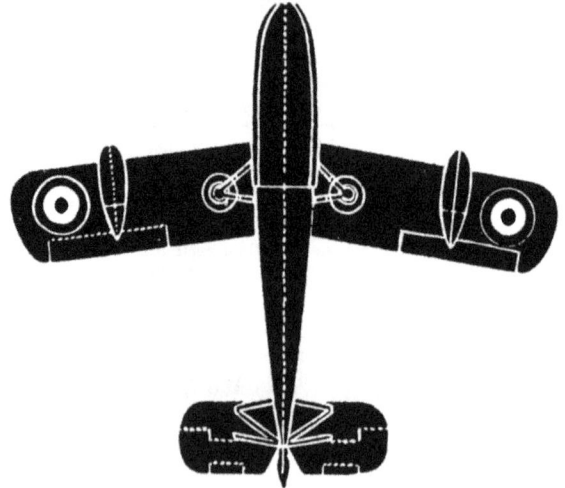

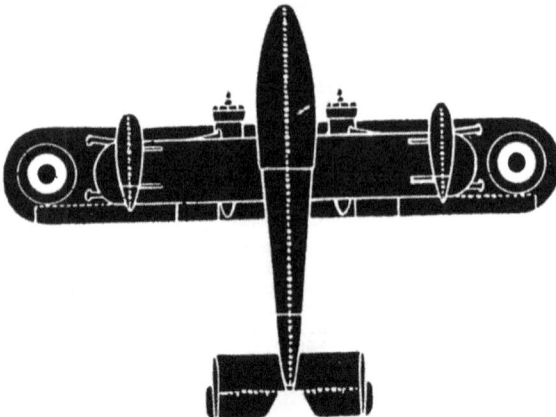

The *Saunders-Roe "London,"* a reconnaissance flying boat with a crew of six, a top speed of 155 m.p.h. and a range of 1,750 miles. Powered by two 1,000-hp. "Pegasus" radial engines. It has gunner's stations in bow, rear cockpit and tail.
Way to Identify — Biplane with wings of unequal span and width. Fuselage underslung on lower wings and two engines underslung on upper. Wings rectangular with semicircular tips. Ribbed two step hull. High rectangular tailplane. Twin fins and rudders.

18

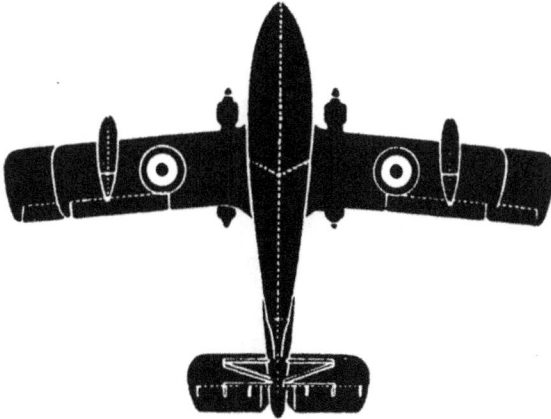

The Short "Singapore," a patrol flying boat with two pairs of Rolls-Royce "Kestrel" engines mounted in tandem, developing altogether 2,600 hp. It has a cruising range of about 1,000 miles and top speed of 150 m.p.h.

Way to Identify—Biplane with wings of unequal span, both wings rectangular and swept back. Tandem engines mounted midway between wings. Three fins and rudders mounted on high braced rectangular tailplane.

The Short "Sunderland," a long-range patrol flying boat that is doing heavy service in the Atlantic patrol. It is powered by four 1,010-hp. Bristol radial engines, and has a top speed of over 200 m.p.h. and a range of 2,900 miles. It has gun turrets in nose and tail and gun positions amidships.

Way to Identify — High-wing monoplane with almost equally tapered wings, having slight dihedral, with fixed wing floats. Large hull of great depth with turret projecting behind tapered tailplane and high single fin and rudder.

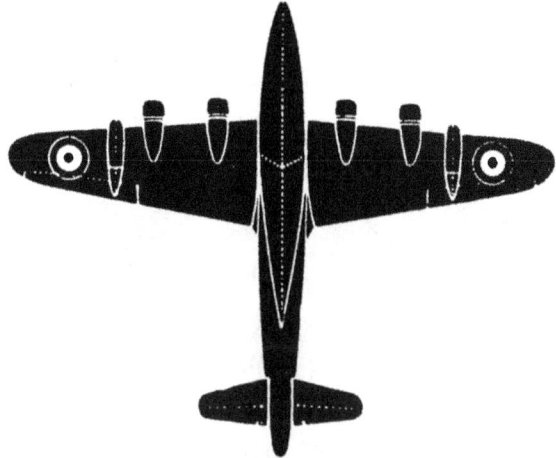

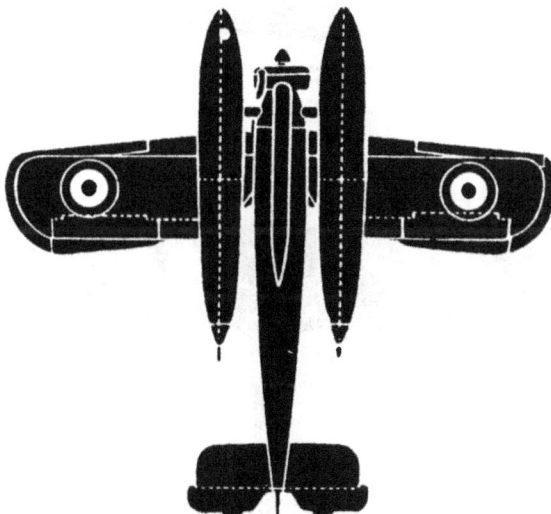

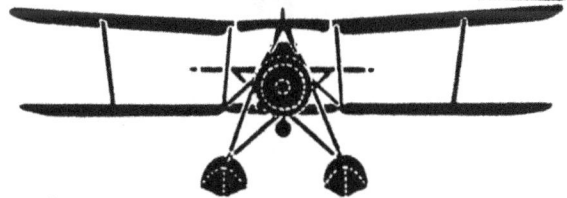

The Fairey "Swordfish," a two- or three-place plane used as a torpedo carrier or reconnaissance. Powered by a Bristol "Pegasus" radial engine of 690-hp., it has a speed of around 155 m.p.h. and mounts a fixed machine gun and a movable machine gun in back cockpit. It is equipped either with pontoons for catapult take-off or landing gear for carrier service.

Way to Identify—Biplane with wings of unequal span and width, the top wing slightly swept back and the narrower bottom wing rectangular. Short cowled nose, twin floats, high tailplane, single fin and rudder.

FRIENDLY PLANES

RUSSIA

The famous "Chato", which made a good show-ing as a fighter against German and Italian planes in Spain. With a stepped-up engine and other modifications, it is now being used as a dive bomber.
Way to Identify—Biplane with wings of unequal span, top wing gull-shape. Short barrel-shape fuselage with single fin and rudder; fixed land-ing gears.

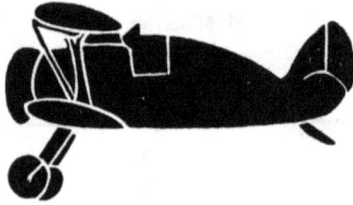

Rata, Russia's standard single-place fighter, the 1-16 "Rata" armed with four machine guns. It is powered by a 700-hp. Wright "Cyclone" engine, and has a top speed of 280 m.p.h. and a cruising range of 500 miles. A later version of this ship, the 1-16B, is powered by a 1,000-hp. M-63 engine and is reported to have a speed of over 300 m.p.h.
Way to Identify—Low mid-wing monoplane with leading edges straight and trailing edges swept forward in unusual way. Short stubby fuselage. Tailplane swept back. Single fin and rudder.

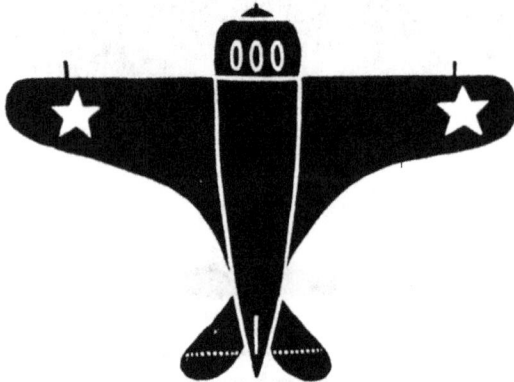

Four-Engine Russian, this is the plane Mazuruk flew to the North Pole with the Schmidt Expedi-tion in 1938. This same type of four-engine mono-plane is said to be used as a bomber in the pres-ent war.
Way to Identify — Low-wing monoplane with wings equally tapered; long, thin fuselage, with windows in nose. Large tailplane with high single fin and rudder. Fixed landing gears.

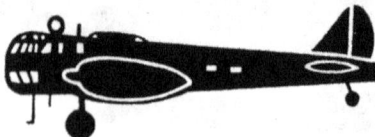

20

The Ark-3 Reconnaissance Flying Boat, powered by two 630-hp. M-25 radial engines. No performance figures available.

Way to Identify — Mid-wing monoplane with wings having sharp dihedral, equally tapered to rounded tips. Thick ark-shape hull with turret in the bow. Tailplane mounted high; single fin and rudder.

Z.K.B.-26, a medium bomber, carries a crew of five, accommodates a bomb of 6,600 lbs. internally. Powered by two 1,000-hp. Gnome-Rhone engines. It has a speed of 310 m.p.h.

Way to Identify — Mid-wing monoplane with wings equally tapered to rounded tips. Transparent nose. Swept back tailplane with high single fin and rudder.

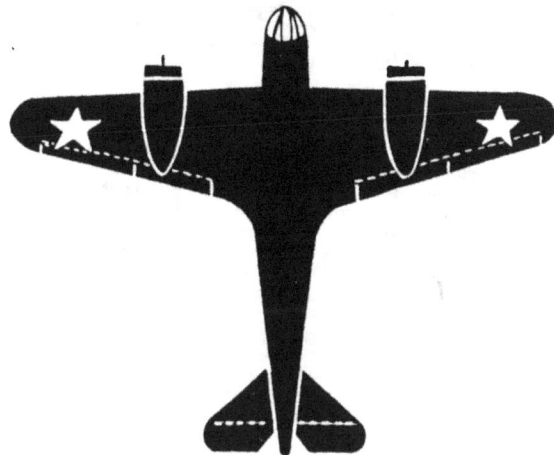

USSR-25, this is the giant single-engine plane, the USSR-25, used for the first trans-polar flight from Moscow to the U.S.A. This plane was reported to be among those used in bombing Berlin.

Way to Identify — High wing monoplane with wings of unusual shape. Long, thin fuselage, large tailplane mounted high with high single fin and rudder.

GERMANY

The Dornier Do. 24, a three-engine reconnaissance flying boat, powered by three B. M. W. radial air-cooled engines of 800-hp. each. It has a speed of 195 m.p.h. and a range of 2,050 miles. It carries three machine guns, and can load twelve 110 pound bombs. Accommodates a crew of six.

Way to Identify — High-wing monoplane with wings swept back on leading edges and square-cut tips. Two step hull with stub wings. Angular braced tailplane, and twin fins and rudders.

The Junkers Ju. 87B, the "Stuka" two-seat dive bomber. It is armed with two machine guns in the wings and a movable machine gun in the rear cockpit. It carries one 1,100 pound bomb under the fuselage, and four 40 pound bombs under the wings. It is powered by a Junkers liquid-cooled engine of 1,200 hp., with a top speed of 250 m.p.h., and a range of about 500 miles.

Way to Identify—Mid-wing monoplane with "inverted gull" wings, slight taper on leading edges, trailing edges swept forward sharply. Large radiator under engine, fixed spatted undercarriage. Rectangular, braced tailplane, large single fin and square-cut rudder.

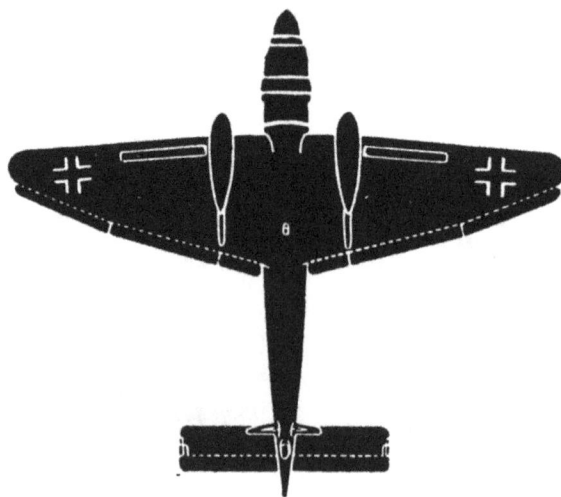

The Messerschmitt Me. 110, a two- or three-seat long-range escort fighter, with two cannon under the nose and four machine guns on top of the nose. This ship has been used in night bombings, carrying a bomb load on external racks. The ship is fitted with two liquid-cooled Daimler-Benz engines of 1,150-hp. each, with a top speed of 365 m.p.h., and a range of 1,150 miles.

Way to Identify — Low-wing monoplane with wings slightly dihedral and uniformly tapered to square tips. Engines nacelles underslung, with radiators beneath, nose projecting in front of engines. Twin fins and rudders.

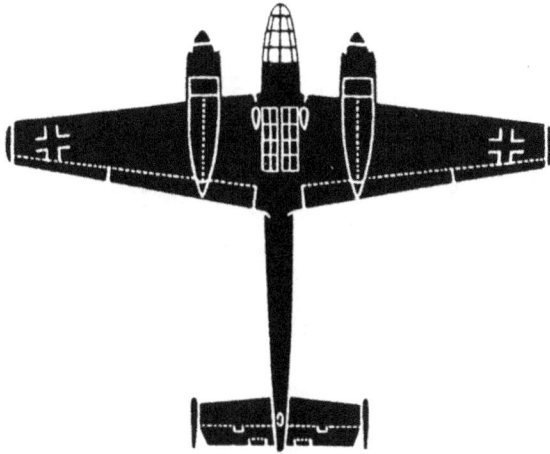

The Messerschmitt "Jaguar," a high-speed, long-range bomber version of the Me. 110 model. The "Jaguar" sacrifices some speed and range to carry half a ton of bombs. It is powered by two 1,150-hp. Daimler-Benz liquid-cooled engines, and carries a crew of four.

Way to Identify — Low-wing monoplane with wings slightly dihedral and uniformly tapered to square tips. Engines nacelles underslung, with radiators beneath, nose projecting in front of engines. Twin fins and rudders, transparent nose.

The Heinkel He. 113, a single-seater fighter in the same class as the Me. 109F, but slightly faster, with a top speed of nearly 400 m.p.h. It is powered by a Daimler-Benz in-line engine of 1,300-hp. There is a cannon mounted on the engine, which fires through the propeller hub, and two machine guns in the wing.

Way to Identify — Low-wing monoplane with wings horizontal at center section, and dihedral on outer sections, which taper to rounded tips. Fuselage rounded with pointed nose. Large tapered tailplane, and single fin and rudder.

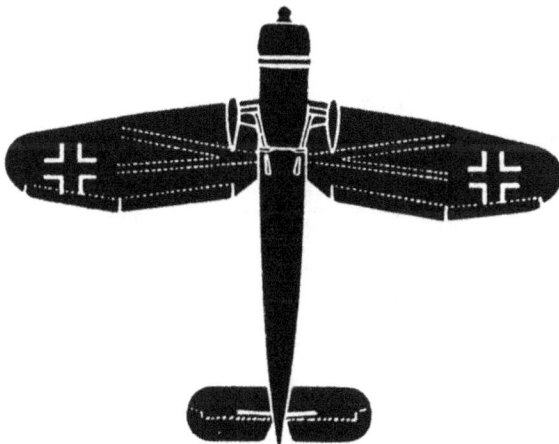

The Henschel Hs. 126, a two-place reconnaissance fighter, armed with a machine gun which fires through the propeller radius, and a flexible machine gun in rear cockpit. It will accommodate either bombs or smoke screen apparatus. The ship is powered by a B. M. W. (Bavarian Motor Works) radial engine of 870-hp., with a top speed of 230 m.p.h., and a range of 685 miles.

Way to Identify — High-wing monoplane with wings braced with V-struts, swept back and cut out at trailing edge in center section. Rounded fuselage, fixed undercarriage with small spatted wheels. Large tailplane braced and mounted high, single fin and rudder.

The Dornier Do. 17, a four-crew medium bomber called "The Flying Pencil" because of its extremely narrow fuselage. It has three machine guns, one in the nose, one on top of the fuselage, and the third under the fuselage. Bombs are carried internally, and also externally on the sides of the fuselage. The ship is fitted with two B. M. W. air-cooled radial engines (as shown), or two liquid-cooled Daimler-Benz engines of 950-hp. each. The top speed is 310 m.p.h., and it has a range of 770 miles.

Way to Identify—High-wing monoplane with thick wings slightly tapered to rounded tips. Long slim fuselage, large engine nacelles, transparent nose extending beyond engines. Twin fins and rudders.

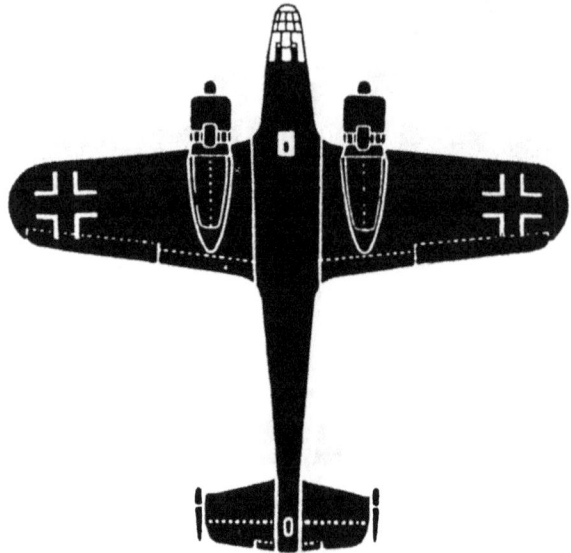

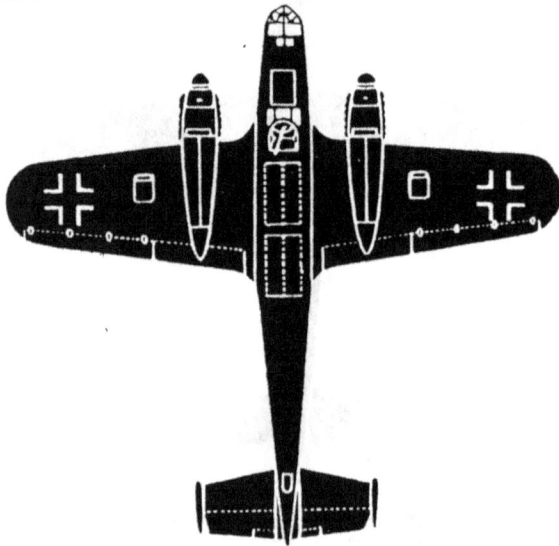

The Dornier Do. 215, a reconnaissance bomber, with three machine guns, one in nose, one on top of fuselage, and the third below. Bombs are carried internally, and also externally on the sides of the fuselage. The ship is fitted with either two radial engines of 700-hp. each, or two liquid-cooled engines of 1,100-hp. each (as shown), which give a reported speed of 335 m.p.h. and a range of nearly 1,000 miles.

Way to Identify — High-wing monoplane, with thick wings slightly tapered to rounded tips. Slim fuselage with paneled nose. Broad tailplane and twin fins and rudders.

The Focke-Wulf Fw. 187 "Zerstorer" (destroyer), a two-seat fighter, one of the recent German designs. It is fitted with either two Daimler-Benz or Junkers engines, and has a top speed of 360 m.p.h. Six machine guns or two cannons are mounted in the nose, and one flexible gun is installed in the rear cockpit.

Way to Identify — Low-wing monoplane, with wings untapered on leading edges, and outer sections of trailing edges swept forward to rounded tips. Thin streamlined fuselage, with large underslung engine nacelles forward of nose. Large single fin and rudder.

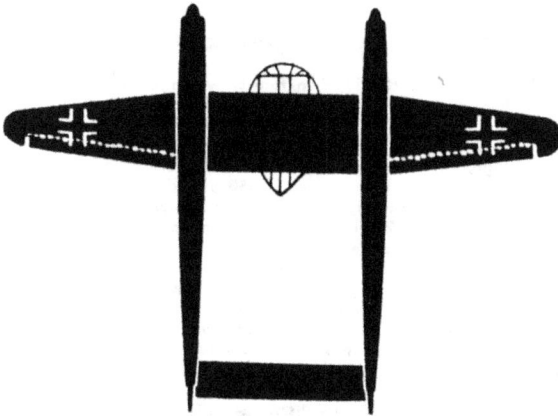

The *Focke-Wulf Fw. 189*, a ground-attack and reconnaissance plane, which carries a crew of three to five. It is powered by two liquid-cooled Daimler-Benz or Junkers engines, and has a top speed of 222 m.p.h. There are two machine guns in the center section of the wings, and guns on top and in the rear of the pilot's nacelle.

Way to Identify — High-wing monoplane, with outer sections of wings tapered. Twin engines forward of transparent nose and thin twin tail-booms. Double fins and rudders.

The *Junkers Ju. 86K*, a diesel-powered four-crew medium bomber, with a speed of 240 m.p.h. and a range of 1,500 miles. The plane pictured is powered with two Junkers Diesel engines of 700-hp., although two B. M. W. radial engines are also standard. It has three machine guns in the nose, and gun stations on upper and under sides of fuselage. Bombs are carried internally.

Way to Identify — Low-wing monoplane, with wings dihedral and uniformily tapered. It has a long nose with transparent front, and underslung engine nacelles. Rectangular braced tailplane, and twin fins and rudders.

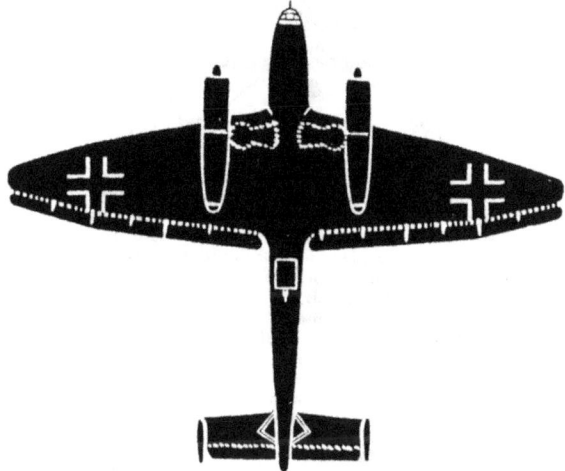

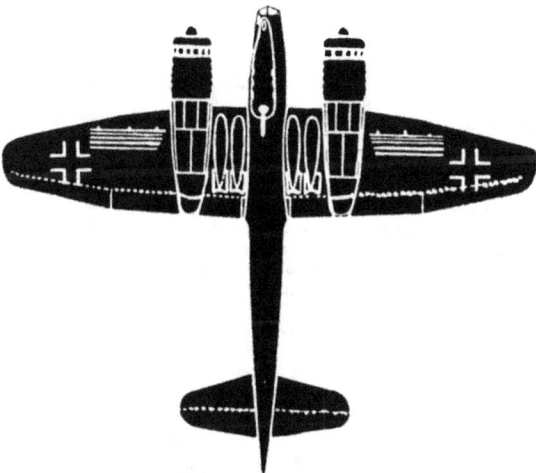

The *Junkers Ju. 88*, a twin-engine dive bomber, first built as a long-range bomber. It became a dive bomber by adding dive brakes and rein-forcing the wings. It is armed with six machine guns, and carries four 550 pound bombs exter-nally under the wings on both sides of fuselage. The ship is fitted with two Junkers 1,200-hp. radial engines, with a speed of 317 m.p.h. and a maximum range of 3,100 miles.

Way to Identify — Low-wing monoplane with dihedral wings, and leading edges swept back on outer sections, trailing edges slightly swept forward to rounded tips. Large underslung engine nacelles, streamlined fuselage with transparent nose. Tapered tailplane, and large single fin and rudder.

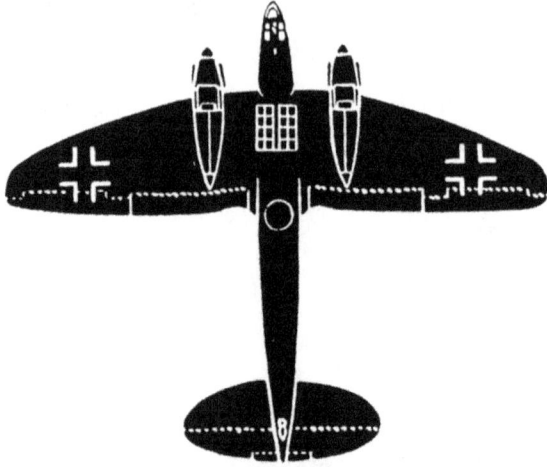

The Heinkel He. 111K, a four-crew long-range heavy bomber that has been used extensively in night raiding over England. It is armed with three machine guns, one in the nose, one on top of fuselage, and the third in a retractable turret under the fuselage. It carries eight 550 pound bombs internally. The ship is powered by two Junkers engines of 1,200-hp., with a top speed of 275 m.p.h. and a range of over 2,600 miles.

Way to Identify — Low-wing monoplane, with wings elliptically swept back on leading edges and trailing edges straight with cut-out at roof. Transparent nose, long and slim. Oval tailplane and a large elliptical single fin and rudder.

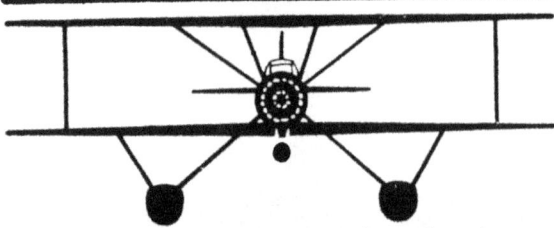

The Arado AR 95, a two-seated torpedo-carrier, reconnaissance and general purpose seaplane (also designed as landplane). It has a machine gun which fires through the propeller radius and a movable machine gun in the observer's cockpit. It carries either a torpedo of 1,760 pounds, a bomb of 1,100 pounds, six 110 pound bombs, or smoke-screen equipment. it is powered by a B. M. W. radial engine of 880-hp.

Way to Identify—Biplane with wings of equal span, with wings swept back and rounded tips. Streamlined fuselage with cowled nose, double floats braced to fuselage by V-shaped struts. Single fin and rudder.

The Blohm and Voss Ha. 142, a four-engine troop transport, which was put into service during the invasion of Norway. It carries thirty armed soldiers and a crew of four. The ship is fitted with four B. M. W. 880-hp. radial engines, with a top speed of 248 m.p.h. and a range of more than 2,700 miles.

Way to Identify — Low-wing monoplane with "inverted gull" wings, rectangular and untapered. Two inner engine nacelles project behind the trailing edges of the wings. Braced rectangular tailplane, and angular twin fins and rudders.

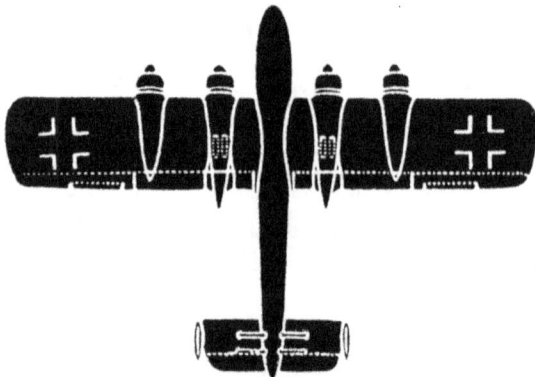

The Blohm and Voss Ha. 140, a twin-engine reconnaissance, torpedo carrier and mine layer seaplane. It has a gun turret in the nose, and a gun station behind the wings. It is fitted with two 880-hp. B. M. W. radial engines, with a speed of 200 m.p.h. and a range of 1,500 miles.

Way to Identify — Mid-wing monoplane with dihedral wings tapered to square-cut tips. Double floats and high braced rectangular tailplane, with circular twin fins and rudders.

The Blohm and Voss Ha. 139, a four-engine seaplane designed for trans-Atlantic flying, now in service as a mine layer. It is fitted with four 600-hp. Junkers diesel engines, with a speed of over 195 m.p.h. and a range of more than 3,000 miles.

Way to Identify — Low-wing monoplane with wings untapered and of the "inverted gull" type with rounded tips Torpedo shaped fuselage, and large fixed twin floats. High braced tailplane, and twin fins and rudders.

The Dornier Do. 26, a long-range reconnaissance flying boat. Though it has a loaded weight of over twenty tons, this ship was designed for catapult launching in trans-Atlantic flying experiments before the war It is fitted with four 600-hp. Junkers water-cooled diesel engines mounted in tandem pairs, with a speed of over 200 m.p.h. and a range of 5,600 miles.

Way to Identify — High-wing monoplane with "gull" wings, swept back at leading edges. Two-step boat hull, tandem nacelles mounted high on wings. Braced high tailplane, and triangular single fin and rudder.

27

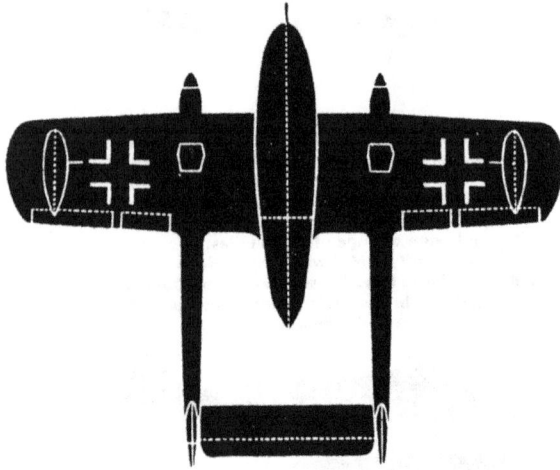

The Blohm and Voss Bv. 138, a three-engine re-connaissance flying boat. It has three gun turrets: a retractable gun turret in the nose, one behind the middle engine, and one in the rear of the hull. It has a speed of approximately 170 m.p.h. and a range of about 1,500 miles.
Way to Identify — High-wing monoplane with wings of slight taper and small dihedral with wide tips. Braced floats near wing tips and short single-step hull. Twin tailbooms with rectangular tailplane and twin fins and rudders.

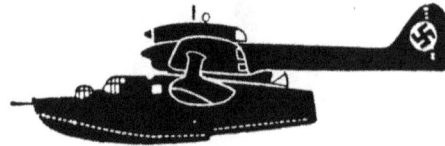

The Focke-Wulf Fw. 200 "Condor," a four-engine troop transport. A plane of this type is used by Hitler for his personal use It is armed with gun turrets in the nose and tail, and accommodates thirty soldiers and a crew of four. It is fitted with four 720-hp. B. M. W. radial engines, with a top speed of 233 m.p.h. and a range of 775 miles. A later version of this ship, used in Atlantic raiding is called the "Kurrier," and is said to carry a crew of six. It is powered by four radial engines of 1,000-hp., giving increased speed and range.
Way to Identify — Low-wing monoplane with wings equally tapered, outer sections dihedral. Four engines with long nacelles and a narrow fuselage. Tapered tailplane and tall single fin and rudder.

The Junkers Ju. 90, Germany's largest landplane, in use as a troop transport. It accommodates forty soldiers and a crew of four. The ship is powered by four B. M. W. engines of 880-hp. or four 1,200-hp. Junkers engines, with a top speed of 236 m.p.h. and a range of 1,300 miles. Model Ju. 89, a bomber, is identical in shape with this ship.
Way to Identify — Low-wing monoplane with dihedral wings swept back strongly on leading edge. Fuselage is deep and slab sided. High-set tailplane and twin fin and rudders.

The Dornier Do. 18K, a reconnaissance flying boat, originally produced as a trans-Atlantic mail carrier, with a range of 5,280 miles. It is powered by two Junkers liquid-cooled Diesel engines of 600-hp. each, and has a speed of 162 m.p.h. It carries a machine gun in nose of hull and one in the hull behind the wings. The ship carries bombs beneath the wings, and accommodates a crew of four.

Way to Identify — High-wing monoplane with wings held on narrow center extension. Wings slightly swept back on leading edges to rounded tips. There are stub wings beneath wings on hull and engines are mounted in tandem on top of wings. Braced tailplane, and single fin and rudder.

The Heinkel He. 115, a three-crew torpedo mine-layer seaplane. It carries two guns and mines, or a 1,760 pound torpedo, and is powered by two B. M. W. 850-hp. radial engines. It has a speed of over 215 m.p.h. and a range of 1,300 miles.

Way to Identify — Mid-wing monoplane, with leading edges swept back to rounded tips. Thin fuselage with a transparent nose, twin floats. Tailplane with leading edges swept back, and single fin and rudder.

The Messerschmitt Me. 109F, Germany's standard single-seat fighter, armed with one cannon and four machine guns. It is powered by a liquid-cooled Daimler-Benz engine of 1,150-hp. with a top speed of 380 m.p.h. and a range of about 700 miles.

Way to Identify — Low-wing monoplane with wings slightly dihedral, and equally tapered to square-cut tips. Fuselage streamlined, with radiator under engine. Tailplane braced and mounted high. Single fin and rudder.

JAPAN

The Kawasaki Army Type 93 Bomber, with a maximum speed of 162 m.p.h. It is powered by two 700-hp. radial engines. No further data available.

Way to Identify — Low-wing monoplane with wings tapered to rounded tips with dihedral on outer sections; whale shape fuselage with windows in nose. Stationary landing gears. Oval twin fins and rudder.

The Mitsubishi "Karigane" MK 11 is a two-place fighter, powered by a 800-hp. radial engine. It is said to have a top speed of 310 m.p.h. and a cruising range of 1,490 miles.

Way to Identify — Low-wing monoplane with wings slightly dihedral and tapered to rounded tips; fuselage tapered with transparent cockpit canopy. Large single fin and rudder.

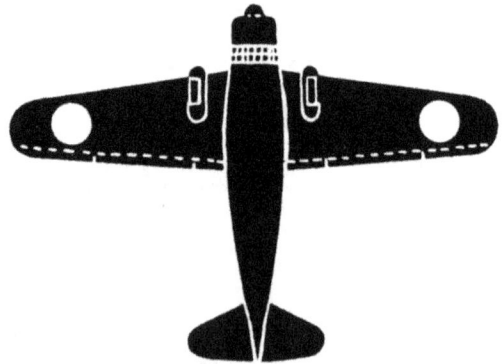

The Mitsubishi "Soyokaze", a long-range bomber that carries a crew of four. It is powered by two 900-hp. radial air-cooled engines. Cruising speed 162 m.p.h.

Way to Identify—Mid-wing monoplane with almost straight leading edges and trailing edges swept forward. Long thin fuselage with turret on top. Tapered tailplane with twin fins and rudder.

30

Nakajima 19, a twin-engine, long-range bomber, powered by two 870-hp. radial air-cooled engines. This ship has a speed of 218 m.p.h. and a range of about 2,500 miles.
Way to Identify — Mid-wing monoplane, with wings equally tapered to rounded tips, long transparent nose extending far in front of engines. Cigar-shape fuselage with large single fin and rudder.

The *Kawanishi 96 Reconnaissance Bomber*, carries bombs externally and has a machine gun in the rear cockpit. The speed is said to be about 200 m.p.h. No other data available.
Way to Identify — Biplane with wings of equal span and unstaggered. Tapered fuselage with cowled radial engine, stationary landing gears, single fin and rudder. Straight tailplane to rounded tips.

The *Nakajima Army Type 94*, a two-place fighter powered by a 550-hp. radial air-cooled engine. It has a top speed of only 187 m.p.h.
Way to Identify — Biplane with wings of unequal span; leading edge straight, trailing edge has slight inward curve. Stationary landing gear. Single fin and rudder.

ITALY

The *Breda 65*, a one- or two-place fighter, or light bomber. As a fighter, it mounts four machine guns in the wings; if used as a bomber, one machine gun is mounted in the rear cockpit, and it carries a bomb load of 12 medium bombs, or 160 light fragmentation bombs. It is powered by a 1,000-hp. Fiat radial engine, and has a speed of 267 m.p.h.

Way to Identify — Low-wing monoplane with dihedral wings swept forward on trailing edges. "Knees" show beneath wings. Nose has crown cowling. Rounded fuselage. Braced tailplane and high single fin and rudder.

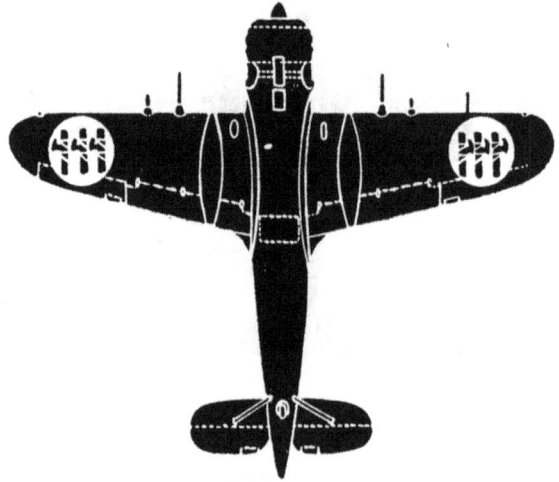

The *Savoia-Marchetti SM. 79*, a three-engine four-crew long-range bomber. It is reported that Italy has more of this type of ship than of any other bomber. It is also said to have poor defensive armament. It carries a bomb load of 2,750 pounds and is fitted with three 1,000-hp. Piaggio radial engines. The top speed is 295 m.p.h., and the cruising range is 1,150 miles.

Way to Identify — Low-wing monoplane with thick tapered wings. Nacelles of two wing engines extend slightly behind trailing edges. One engine in the nose. Deep slab-sided fuselage. Half rounded tailplane, and curved single fin and rudder.

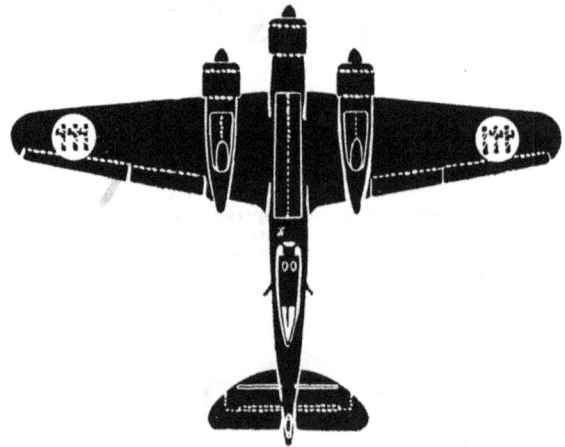

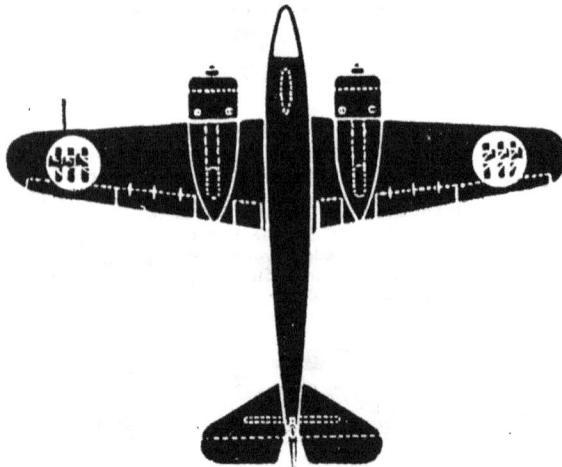

The *Savoia-Marchetti SM-85*, Italy's new single-seat twin-engine dive bomber. It is fitted with two Piaggio 1,000-hp. engines, and has a maximum speed of 315 m.p.h. This ship is reported to have made a very poor showing in actual use.

Way to Identify—High mid-wing monoplane with dihedral tapered wings. Slab-sided fuselage with a curved "belly." Braced tailplane swept back on leading edges, and high single fin and rudder.

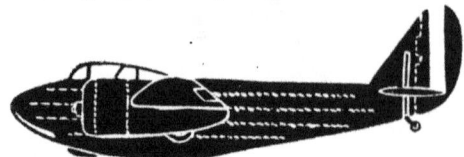